Netball

Written in association
with England Netball

Produced for A & C Black by

Monkey Puzzle Media Ltd
Little Manor Farm, The Street
Brundish, Woodbridge, Suffolk IP13 8BL

Published in 2009 by

A & C Black Publishers Ltd
36 Soho Square, London W1D 3QY
www.acblack.com

Fifth edition 2009

ISBN: 978 07136 7697 6

A CIP catalogue record for this book is available
from the British Library.

Acknowledgements
Cover and inside design by James Winrow and
Tom Morris for Monkey Puzzle Media Ltd.
Cover photograph © England Netball.
Inside photographs © England Netball.
Illustrations by Dave Saunders.

With many thanks to Linda Swain, Sheelagh Redpath
and Reena Lathia from England Netball.

Printed and bound in China by C&C Offset
Printing Co., Ltd.

CONTENTS

INTRODUCTION

Netball is a popular international sport that involves throwing and catching a ball. The game is played on a comparatively small hard court area between two teams of seven players. Each team aims to score goals by throwing the ball through a ring attached to a goalpost at each end of the court.

This young player tries to get the ball!

PARTICIPATION

Netball is traditionally played by women, although the rules allow for men to participate, provided the game is single sex. For young players of primary-school age, the 5-a-side game 'High Five' is recommended; in this, girls and boys play in the same team.

Netball is a good game for many people with a disability. With minor modifications to the rules with regard to mobility, equipment and decision-making, it can offer the rewards of sociability, teamwork, fitness and fun to almost anyone who wants to take part.

SKILLS

High-level physical skills are needed because of the following features of netball:

- restrictions in the playing area

- rules controlling footwork

- non-contact nature of the sport.

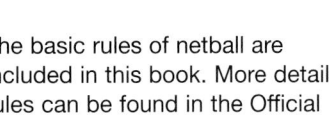

The top players need speed, strength and balance.

The basic rules of netball are included in this book. More detailed rules can be found in the Official Netball Rules book (available from England Netball, Netball House, 9 Paynes Park, Hitchin, Herts, SG5 1EH, Telephone: (01462) 442344 and at www.england-netball.co.uk).

Netball is an easy game to organise as it does not require a large quantity of equipment.

BEFORE YOU GET GOING

What do you need to start a game of netball? This section explains, with information on the court, the type of ball used, clothing and the length of each game.

THE COURT

A full-sized netball court should be 30.5m long and 15.25m wide and the surface needs to be firm and non-slip. Top players use their feet in a very precise, controlled way, with sudden stops and turns. A loose, soft or soggy playing surface is dangerous, and would not allow the footwork netball requires.

The measurements for a full-sized netball court, plus the names of the different parts of the court. Lines are considered part of the court, which only ends at their outside edge. If an on-court player's foot is on the line, she or he is still in play. Court lines must be no more than 50mm wide.

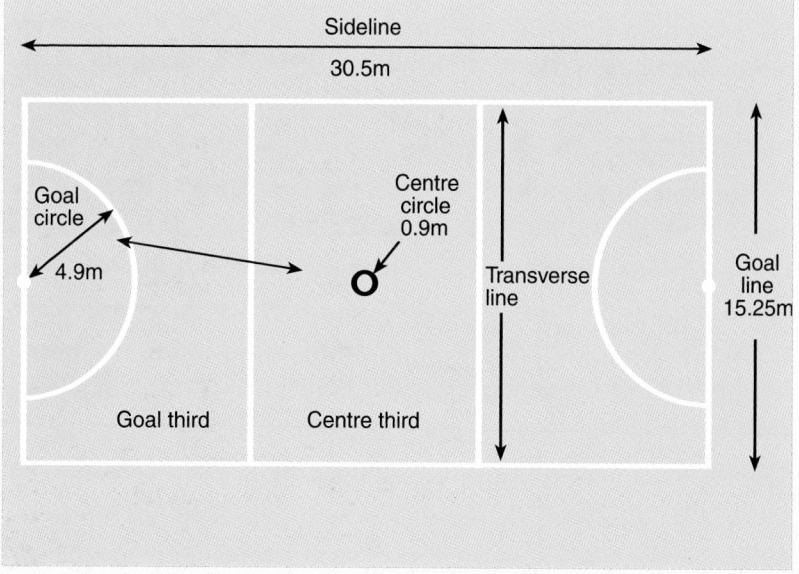

THE GOALPOST

The goalpost is a vertical pole that is inserted into a socket in the ground or supported by a metal base. It must be 3.05m high with a diameter of 65mm–100mm. It is positioned in the centre of the goal line so that the back of the post is at the outside of the line.

The ring through which a goal is scored extends 150mm from the top of the post. It has an internal diameter of 380mm and is fitted with a net that is open at both ends. Both the ring and net are considered to be part of the goalpost.

THE BALL

• A size 5 netball is made from leather, rubber or a similar material.

• It is 690mm–710mm in circumference and weighs 400g–450g.

Test a netball by applying pressure with your fingers to the surface of the ball. There should be little indentation if it is properly inflated.

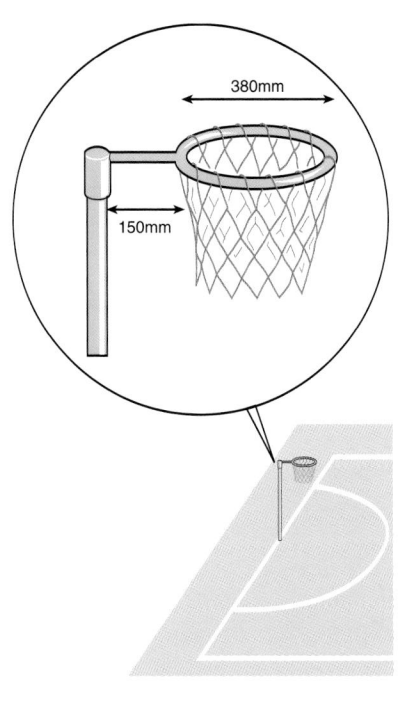

380mm

150mm

Position and dimensions of the goalpost.

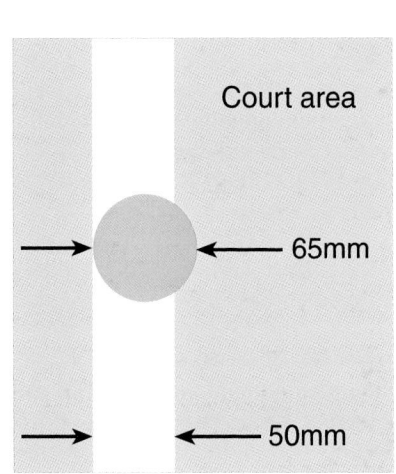

Court area

65mm

50mm

 A full team consists of twelve players.

CLOTHING

Players must display the initials of their playing position (e.g. GA) on both front and back, above the waist, in letters 150mm high. Registered matching team uniforms are required in a formal match, and it is good to be able to identify each other quickly during a competitive game.

Netball kit can incorporate the latest technological, fashionable and fun trends in sportswear, but needs to provide ease of movement, absorbency and warmth.

THE PLAYERS

A team consists of twelve players, but only seven of these are on court at any one time.

- Substitutions are allowed during play, although a game may be played if only five or six players from a team are on court.
- Each playing position is confined to a limited area of the court. A player venturing outside of her or his area is offside.
- All players need similar basic skills, but their playing positions emphasise some of these skills more than others.

In order to prevent injury, jewellery is not permitted on court. For the same reason, finger-nails must be cut short and hair tied back.

 Netball clothing incorporates the latest designs in sportswear.

SHOES

Footwear is the most important item of clothing. Shoes should be made of light-weight material and provide comfort, support and durability. Spiked soles are not permitted.

THE CLOCK

- A netball match lasts for 60 minutes of play.

- This is divided into four quarters of 15 minutes each.

- Intervals of 3 minutes are taken between the first/second, and third/fourth quarters, with an interval of 5 minutes at half-time.

- Teams change ends after each quarter.

SHORTER GAMES

The length of a netball game can be altered, for instance when teams play more than one match in a day. In this case two halves of 20 minutes with a 5-minute interval at half-time is suggested.

During one-day tournaments or in games between young players, games may vary from 7 minutes for each half to 15 minutes; alternatively, four quarters of 9, 10 or 12 minutes can be played.

Official timekeepers watch the clock in international matches.

9

PLAYING POSITIONS

As with every team sport, netball players take up specific positions on the court. Each player has a particular job to do: in successful teams, every single player on the court contributes to each score.

GS (GOAL SHOOTER)

- Main job is to score goals.
- Confined to a small playing area.
- Uses less energy than other players but needs stamina to concentrate on shooting.

GA (GOAL ATTACK)

- Scores goals and assists attack in the goal third to move the ball towards the goal circle.
- Also contributes to attack in the centre third.

WA (WING ATTACK)

- Tries to receive the ball at the centre pass, by moving into the centre third, before taking another pass in the attacking goal third to offer a pass into the circle.
- Continually sprinting, dodging and moving onto the ball in the goal third.
- Must also have the energy to help in the centre third.

TACTICAL TEAMWORK

Experience, coaching and planning will alter the patterns of teamwork in attack and defence. However, these tactical switches cannot change the main emphasis of a player's job, which is dictated by the rule concerning playing positions.

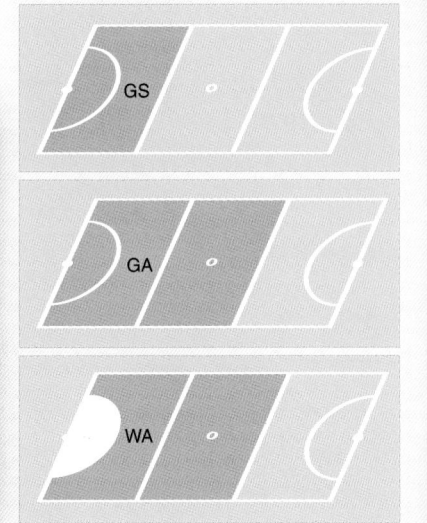

C (CENTRE)

- Contributes to attack and defence in all areas of the court except the circles.

- Needs to have huge stamina.

- Also needs good observation to decide when to receive the ball and when to move to create space for a player in a better position.

WD (WING DEFENCE)

- Main job is to defend the opposing WA.

- Must mark to stop the WA's dodging moves and defend the ball to upset the opposition passing.

GD (GOAL DEFENCE)

- Main job is similar to that of the WD, with the added area of the goal circle to cover.

- Must anticipate opposing GA's intentions in order to stop their movement towards the goal.

- Needs the specialist skill of defending a shot for goal.

GK (GOAL KEEPER)

- Main job is to defend – and defend again and again!

- Tries to prevent opponents from receiving the ball.

- Defends shots at goal as a second line of defence.

- Retrieves missed shots under the post as a third line of defence.

- Must make accurate passes out of the goal circle.

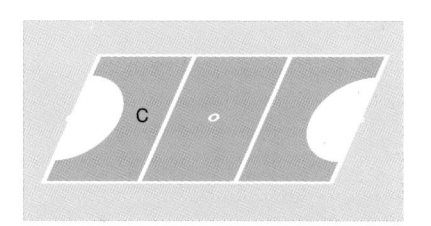

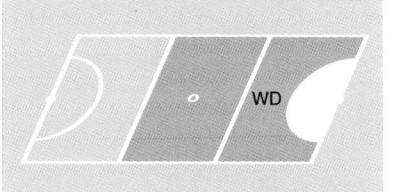

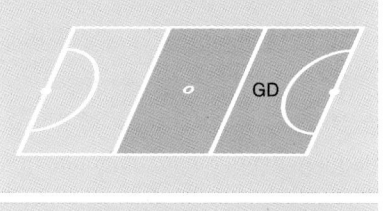

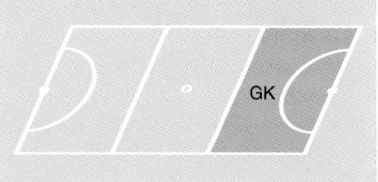

One of the world's best goal shooters, Australia's Catherine Cox. **11**

GAME ON!

Before the start of a game, the captains toss a coin to determine which team will have the choice of the first centre pass or the goal end into which they will shoot. Then the game is ready to begin! This section looks at how the umpire begins play, explaining the centre pass. When one of the teams scores a goal, play stops and is restarted.

START OF PLAY – CENTRE PASS

Before the start of play, only the two centres may be in the centre third. All other players may be in any part of their own goal third.

The game starts with a centre pass taken by the centre of the team in possession of the ball. This centre must be standing inside the centre circle, though one foot may be off the ground. The opposing centre may be standing or moving anywhere inside the centre third without causing an obstruction.

After the umpire blows the whistle for the centre pass, the ball must be caught within the centre third by any one of the four players in the figure. These players can start from any point along the transverse line or within their goal third and may move in any direction to land at any point within the centre third.

FIRST PASSAGE OF PLAY

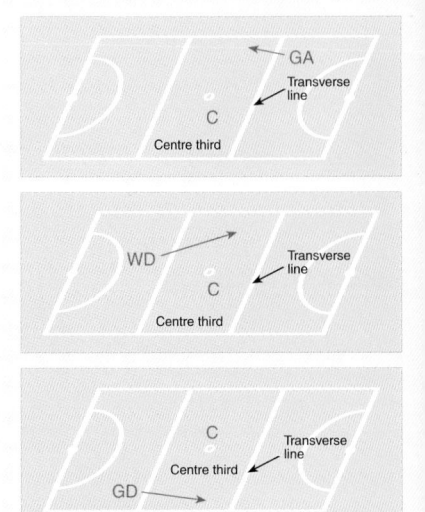

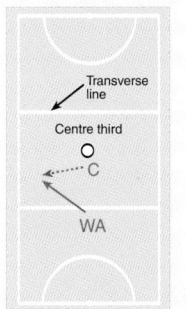

ATTACKING PHASE

Following a completed centre pass, a pattern of passing develops, moving the ball to one of the shooters in the circle. Many different passing patterns will be used during the game, two of which are illustrated below.

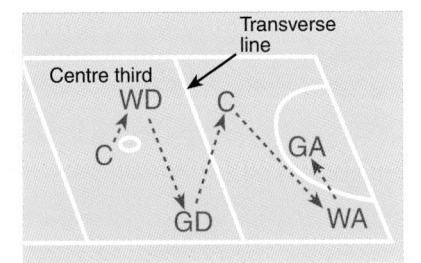

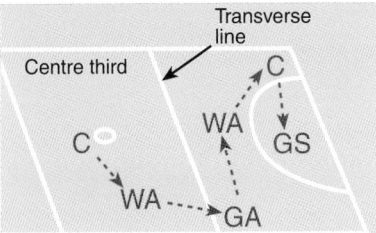

Passing patterns following a completed centre pass.

SHOOTING
As soon as the GS or the GA has the ball in the goal circle she or he is allowed to take a shot for goal or pass the ball again if a clear shot is not possible.

If a defending player intercepts the centre pass, play continues.

RESTART
If a shot is successful, the game returns to the line-up for the start of play. A centre pass, which is taken alternately by the two centres, restarts the game.

RULES FOR STARTING PLAY

There should be two umpires, one on either sideline. Each umpire controls the half of the court to their right of the centre circle, plus their own sideline. Umpires do not change sides of the court during the match.

- At the start of play, players may not move into the centre third before the whistle is blown.

- It is the responsibility of the centre to wait until all the players are onside, before stepping into the centre circle to take the centre pass. The umpire will then blow the whistle to start play.

- If two players from opposite sides simultaneously break this rule, the umpire plays on unless either touches the ball, in which case a toss-up is taken.

The centre
When the whistle is blown, the centre with the ball must release it within 3 seconds and must obey the footwork rule described on page 12.

The first pass

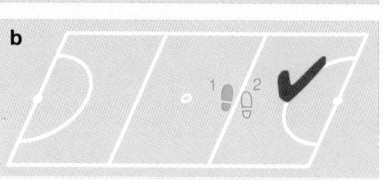

a

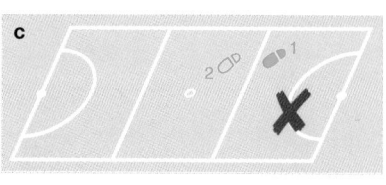

b

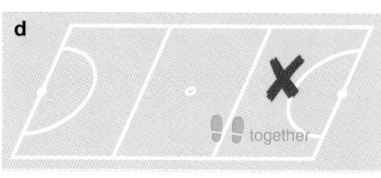

c

d

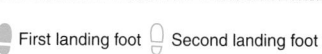

Receiving the centre pass means either catching the ball or touching it. When receiving a centre pass, a player can land in the centre third (**a**) or with one foot only just inside the centre third as long as it is the first landing foot (**b**). Landing first on one foot in the goal third is not permitted even if the second foot subsequently lands in the centre third (**c**). Landing on both feet astride the transverse line is also not permitted (**d**).

First landing foot   Second landing foot

HIGH-FIVE NETBALL

The official 5-a-side netball for primary schools (ages 9–11 years), High-Five provides the link to the full 7-a-side game. The rules have been modified to allow players greater freedom around the court and give them more time in which to make their decisions and to act upon them. The game encourages maximum participation from those involved and introduces the roles of scorers, timekeepers and centre pass markers. It is designed for friendly matches, local and area festivals, school or club leagues, coaching sessions and holiday play schemes.

The game is played on a full-sized court with the same markings and the only equipment variation is:
• size 4 netball
• goalpost 2.74m.

The other minor alterations to the game are:
• 7–9 players in a squad
• players rotate
• four quarters of 6 minutes
• 4 seconds to pass or shoot
• no outstretched arms to defend the ball.

FREE PASS

A free pass is awarded for any fault in receiving the centre pass, except that a throw-in is awarded if the ball goes out of court over the sideline bounding the centre third.

The landing point is not important if a defending player is the first to touch or catch the centre pass; play continues.

KNOW THE SKILLS – SHOOTING

One of the basic skills of netball is shooting. Players must learn to shoot by paying attention to the rule on footwork. They must also exercise the skills needed to complete a successful shot: finding a good position, aiming high, maintaining balance and focus.

RESPONDING TO PLAY

Speedy response to play in the goal area is the key to being a good GS or GA. Here are some details on the shooting rule to increase players' awareness:

1. If either shooter wins the ball in a toss-up in the circle, they may choose to shoot or pass.

2. If a free pass is taken by a shooter standing within the circle, a pass and not a shot for goal must be made.

3. If a penalty pass or shot is awarded to the shooting team within the circle, either player can take the ball and choose whether to shoot or pass.

4. A penalty pass/shot is awarded to the shooting team if a shot at goal is disrupted because a defending player moves the goalpost.

5. A goal is scored if a shot goes through the ring, even if a defending player touches the ball in the air.

6. If the whistle for 'time' is blown just after a penalty pass/shot is awarded, the shot is still taken.

7. If the ball travels over and through the ring from a pass by any other player from any other position, no goal is scored. Play continues from where the ball is caught.

8. When the whistle is blown for 'time' after a shot has been made, a goal is scored only if the ball has passed completely through the ring, though not necessarily out of the net.

9. When the ball is out of court and a throw-in is awarded to the attacking team, GS or GA must take the throw-in if it is awarded at any point behind the line bounding the goal circle.

When shooting, players must observe all other rules of play, including footwork, playing the ball, obstruction and contact.

WHEN TO SHOOT

- A player must be completely within the goal circle to shoot.

- When preparing to shoot, a player must not make contact with the ground outside the circle either when catching the ball or while holding it.

- If a shooter is standing on the line, or leans on the ball while it is on the ground in the court area outside the circle, they may recover and shoot. If this happens behind the goal line the ball is considered to be out of court.

MISSED SHOTS

Players may retrieve their own missed shot and shoot again, as long as the attempted shot has touched any part of the goalpost, including the net. Players may also retrieve another shooter's miss and shoot immediately.

Players who know the shooting rule well can move quickly to retrieve a missed 'shot'. There will be no umpire's whistle to guide them.

SHOOTING TECHNIQUES

For shooting, take up a balanced position, feet hip-width apart, back straight.

- Line body up to face the goal, holding the ball high above head with dominant hand under the ball, fingers facing back using second hand to steady the ball if necessary.

- Lower ball over and behind the head, flexing but not lowering the elbow and wrist.

- Use knees and the ankles to help push ball upwards and forwards.

- Fingers follow through facing ring, trajectory high with ball dropping into the ring.

Too much speed in the upward extension of the arms and fingers will cause the ball to fly over the ring.

AIM HIGH

It is necessary to lift high before making any forward movement. A good defender will limit the space within which the shooter's arm can move, without making contact with the ball.

A good, balanced position is important for shooting.

GOOD SHOT

When completing a shot, the forward movement is made almost exclusively by the wrist through to the fingers in shots taken near the post, and from the elbow through the forearm first when more power is required.

FIND A GAP

Shooters who are being closed down by a good defender's long reach and forward lean may step sideways or backwards before shooting. This increases the space for shooting. However, balance is more difficult and it is even more important to emphasise the vertical body position and arm movement before releasing the ball.

SHOOTING TECHNIQUE

These photos demonstrate good shooting technique. Notice some of the following:

- position of the feet
- the fingers – whether holding, supporting or pushing the ball
- vertical body positions
- focus of the shooter's eyes, which look just above and to the back of the ring and not at the defender's hand.

OFFSIDE/OUT OF COURT

Players must be aware of their movements on court, paying particular attention to playing areas. They must know what happens if they go offside or the ball goes out of court.

OFFSIDE

Players must remain in their playing area (see pages 10 and 11) and are offside if they go elsewhere on the court. A player who is in an offside position is penalised.

Umpires are not required to note and evaluate whether the offside player:

- is holding or has touched the ball

- has gone offside deliberately or accidentally

- has wholly entered the offside area or has only a small part of one foot offside

- enters momentarily or remains offside.

In all of these situations, the player is offside and the opposing team is given a free pass at the point in the offside area where the player first crossed the boundary line, unless it puts the non-offending team at a disadvantage.

A player may be ruled offside when taking a throw-in if they step behind an offside area while still in possession of the ball.

 It is important to ensure you are not offside when taking a throw-in.

BOTH OFFSIDE

Two players near each other, working to get free or defending in order to get the ball, may both go offside. The following rules apply:

- If neither player catches or touches the ball, there is no penalty and play continues.

- If either player catches or touches the ball, a toss-up is taken between them in their onside area.

- If both players catch or touch the ball, a toss-up is taken.

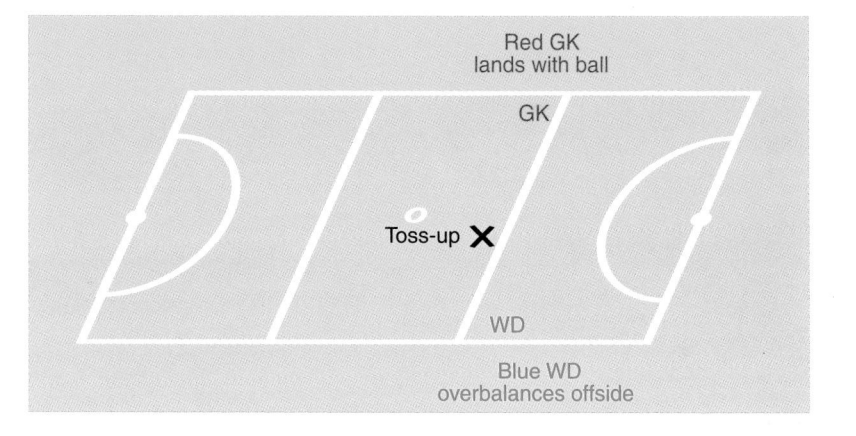

Toss-up ✕

C — Red centre runs offside

WA — Blue WA catching ball

▲ Occasionally, two players may not be close but may both be offside. In this case, a toss-up in their area at a point mid-way between them is taken.

Red GK lands with ball

GK

Toss-up ✕

WD

Blue WD overbalances offside

REACH OUT

The ball cannot be offside, so a player can reach from their onside area to pick up or lean on the ball in an offside area as long as they do not touch the ground.

▲ In a rare situation, the two offside players do not have a common playing area. As one has the ball, a penalty is awarded, but in this case is taken between any two opposing players allowed in the area where the toss-up should be taken.

21

OUT OF COURT

The ball is out of court if it touches the ground, touches an object such as a wall, tree or person who is in contact with the ground, or is in the hands of a player touching the ground out of court.

For all out of court decisions, a throw-in is given to the opposing team from where the ball left the court.

AIRBORNE PASSES

Air space beyond the court area is not regarded as out of court. Therefore, a player can stand on court and lean sideways to retrieve a ball in the air above the ground out of court. Players can also jump from inside the court and bat the ball in the air outside the court area. If the ball arrives back on the court, play will continue even if the player lands outside.

Pushing to the limit!

OUT OF COURT PLAYER

A player is out of court when in possession of the ball and one of the conditions for the ball being out of court applies. Attacking players can stand or move out of court for tactical reasons but have to re-enter the court before trying to play the ball. Defending players must be within the court in order to take defending action.

If two opposing players jump and catch the ball at the same time, but one lands out of court, a toss-up is taken on court between the two players.

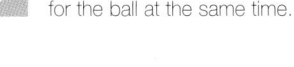
These two young players are jumping for the ball at the same time.

BACK IN THE GAME

A player who leaves the court to get the ball or take a throw-in must be allowed back on to the court near to that spot. The penalty for attempting to prevent an opponent from re-entering the court is a penalty pass or a penalty pass/shot on court where the defending player was standing.

ON THE LINE
• A player is not out of court when standing on the line.
• Because the goalpost is on the line, a ball which hits the post is not out of court if it rebounds back on court.

KNOW THE SKILLS – CATCHING

One of the primary skills of netball is catching, and players must learn to execute good catching skills within the rules, particularly those relating to footwork.

THE CATCHING RULE

A player is permitted to catch the ball with one or both hands. Before catching the ball, the player may bat or bounce it once, or tip the ball in an uncontrolled manner once or more than once. This is most likely to occur when two players are attempting to catch a ball in the air.

KEEPING POSSESSION

Having caught or held the ball, a player may not drop the ball and replay it. 'Replay' means the player may neither catch the ball again, nor bat/bounce it for someone else in the team to catch or retrieve.

FOOTWORK FOR CATCHING

A player can receive the ball while one or both feet are on the ground, or jump to catch and land on one or both feet. Following a catch, only one more complete step is allowed, though the landing foot may be lifted before throwing the ball.

GOOD CATCHING TECHNIQUE

- Anticipate the catch – stretch or jump to reach the ball early.
- Cover a large area of the ball – spread and curve the fingers.
- Absorb the speed of the ball – let your body 'give' by bending the arms slightly.
- Anticipate the landing – if this is with one foot, thrust it towards the ground but prepare to bend on contact. The second foot can be used to complete the balance or to assist a body swerve into the direction of the following throw.

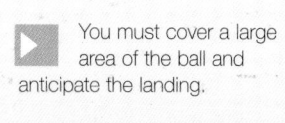
You must cover a large area of the ball and anticipate the landing.

When making a one-handed catch, quickly bring the other hand on to the ball for extra security.

POOR CATCHING TECHNIQUE

- Unsafe hands will cause fumbling, resulting in bouncing/batting more than once or replaying the ball, which are not allowed.

- Poor timing in preparation for the catch is likely to lead to loss of balance.

- Poor anticipation during the catch will affect control of footwork after landing.

 A great one-handed catch.

 A two-footed landing can be attempted if a player is well balanced in the air.

GETTING THE BALL

While preparing to catch, a player can do the following:

- Gain control of the ball if it rebounds from any part of the goalpost, including the net. This rule usually applies to a shooter or defender trying to gain or regain possession of the ball after a missed shot. However, a badly thrown ball will sometimes hit the post and rebound elsewhere on the court.

- Reach towards a ball on the ground and roll it in order to pick it up.

While preparing to catch, a player cannot do the following:

- Attempt to gain possession while lying, sitting or kneeling on the ground, or by deliberately falling on the ball.

- Step outside the court and jump from this position to catch the ball before landing inside the court.

- Hold on to the goalpost for support while reaching for the ball.

The goal attack and goal defence both want to get the ball.

HOLDING THE BALL AND POSSESSION

Once in possession of the ball, a player can lean on the ball on the ground, as long as it is on the court and even if it is in an offside area. Once in possession of the ball, a player cannot do the following:

- Keep possession for more than 3 seconds.

- Lean on the goalpost.

- Throw the ball while lying, sitting or kneeling on the ground. A fallen player must regain their footing and throw within 3 seconds of catching the ball.

- Roll the ball to another player.

- Release the ball, either accidentally or deliberately, and replay it; this includes the drop mentioned on page 24, and a toss, bounce, or throw replayed by the same player. It also applies to a missed shot which has not touched the goalpost.

NO GO!

Players are not allowed to strike the ball with their fist, deliberately kick the ball (although the ball is allowed to hit a player's leg accidentally and rebound), or use the goalpost for any action other than shooting.

The umpire blows the whistle to stop the game.

KNOW THE SKILLS – THROWING

The footwork rule requires good players to exercise a remarkable degree of control considering the speed at which they will run, turn and catch in the course of a game. It also applies when players are performing another basic skill of netball, throwing.

THE FOOTWORK RULE

The footwork rule dictates that after completing a catch with just one foot on the ground, a player may step with the other foot in any direction, lift the landing foot and throw or shoot before this foot is re-grounded.

SPEED AND DISTANCE

Powerful throwing can move the ball quickly down the court, and a good throwing technique requires players to work within the limits of the footwork rule.

To achieve throwing power, a player should start with more weight on the back foot and take a driving step forward on to the front foot, transferring weight in conjunction with the forward thrust of the arm.

Lifting the landing foot may occur naturally as a result of the forward drive, but care must be taken not to drag this foot. A player will be penalised for dragging or sliding the landing foot.

> The actions of the front and back foot when throwing are determined by the footwork rule and technical accuracy.

This wing attack moves the ball down the court with a powerful throw.

A player pivots
with the ball.

ONE OR TWO FEET?

For a right-handed player, landing
on the right foot followed by the
left foot is a better base for a good
throw. If the player lands on the
left foot, the same rules on
footwork apply.

A player who lands on two feet
may choose which foot to move.
As soon as one foot is lifted, the
other is treated as the landing foot.

PIVOTING

- A player may pivot on the
  landing foot and step
  with the other foot in
  any direction any
  number of times.

- The pivoting foot may
  be lifted, but the player
  must throw or shoot
  before re-grounding it.

BALANCING ACT

To achieve balance after landing, less skilled players will step on to the other foot almost immediately. If you are still not balanced, keep the right foot firmly on the ground and take small steps with the left until you are steady.

When facing the wrong way for a throw, keep the right foot down to act as a pivot, and turn by taking steps with the left.

DIRECTION

Be prepared to adjust the direction of a throw to pass it to a receiver who has found some space. Pivoting contributes to this skill. Skilled players will retain their balance on both feet until required to pass in response to the signals of other players. To pass accurately, in your final step, the left foot should point to where the ball is directed.

The wing attack passes the ball.

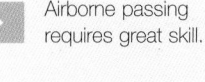
Airborne passing requires great skill.

A player may jump from the landing foot on to the other foot and jump again, but must throw the ball or shoot before re-grounding either foot.

GET SOME AIR!

It requires great skill from a player who is airborne to recognise from the positioning and movement of other players that it's possible to land, gain ground and throw without stopping.

An airborne pass is exceptionally fast. The right foot lands and is used as a springboard for an immediate jump on to the left foot, which is itself a springboard for a jump while throwing. Synchronised with the footwork, the arms are preparing for the appropriate throw.

Jumps may be dramatically high, but it is more usual for the first to be a 'bound', like a very springy running step.

GAINING GROUND

The footwork described above can be used when taking a free pass or a penalty shot in order to be nearer the receiver or the goalpost. Stand on the spot indicated, and deliberately jump forwards before throwing or shooting.

GET SOME AIR! (Cont.)

A player may step with the non-landing foot and jump, but must throw the ball. Here, the step is likely to be just a preparation into the jump, because a thrower wants to rise above a defending player.

The throw requires very fast arm movements, since the preparation and movement into release of the ball must be achieved while the player is still airborne.

FOOTWORK FACTS

- While in possession of the ball, players cannot jump from one foot and land on the same foot (hop).

- A player cannot jump from two feet and land back on two, but can land on one.

- For footwork faults, a free pass is taken from the point of the incorrect step or jump or where a slide started.

- When a free pass, or any other penalty, is taken, the player must obey the footwork rule after standing in position on two feet close to the spot indicated by the umpire.

- A player responding to an umpire's whistle to restart play is not called for footwork until after the whistle has been blown, e.g. the centre at a centre pass.

IN THE AIR – DRILL

A good training drill is to have players standing on a bench, in possession of the ball. Each player jumps off the bench and passes the ball accurately to a moving player before landing on the ground.

Throwing the ball while airborne requires fast movement.

PLAYING THE BALL

After catching the ball a player may:

- throw it in any manner and in any direction to another player
- bounce it with one or both hands in any direction to another player.

Before catching the ball a player can:

- direct it by batting or bouncing it towards another player.

After one bounce or bat, or tipping the ball in an uncontrolled manner, a player can direct it to another player by batting or bouncing it as before.

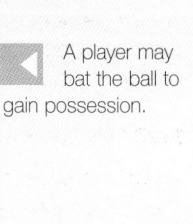

A player may bat the ball to gain possession.

KNOW THE SKILLS – PASSING

The rule on throwing limits the maximum and minimum distance that the ball can travel. It cannot be thrown over a whole third of the court. Players must therefore be able to perform good long and short passes.

LONG PASS

The ball cannot be thrown over a whole third of the court, crossing two transverse lines. Therefore, the maximum distance required for a pass during play is likely to be no more than that shown below.

A long pass.

GOOD TECHNIQUE

This player demonstrates a good long pass technique. Her feet are placed in such a way as to allow for the transference of weight described on page 28. Her arm is well drawn back, giving space for a long thrust forwards while gathering speed to produce power, and this movement will include the rotation to bring the right shoulder forwards.

A final accelerating flick from the wrist as if her fingers are trying to push through the ball adds power, while the follow-through should be exaggerated to pinpoint the direction of the pass.

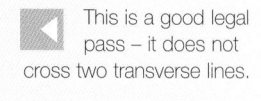

This is a good legal pass – it does not cross two transverse lines.

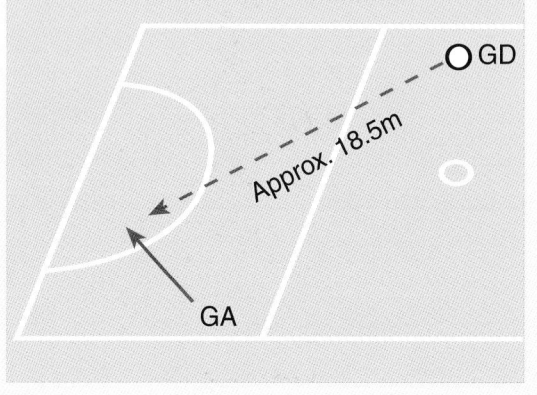

Approx. 18.5m

GD

GA

A rapid backward movement just before releasing a long pass helps to make the ball 'stick' to the hand.

SHORT PASS

Passes must travel a minimum distance. At the moment the ball is passed, there must be room for a third player to move between the hands of the thrower and those of the receiver. This rule is somewhat imprecise, and requires the umpire to decide what is 'room to move' and watch the players' hands closely.

The rule allows space for defenders to attempt interceptions without making contact but means that players can be very close when passing.

GOOD TECHNIQUE

Short passes require precision and delicacy. Notice this player's wrist and finger movements.

The three stages of a short chest pass.

FIVE PASSING POINTERS

The best passing advice for new netball players is to learn to pass with either hand or both hands. Here are some other passing pointers:

- Change the power of a pass by increasing or decreasing the strength of movements and the amount of body involvement.

- Try to anticipate the direction as well as the force required for a pass.

- Control the direction of the flight of the ball by adjusting the point of release, by stepping to face the aiming point and by following through in that direction.

- Aim at a point in space where the receiver will arrive by the time the ball has travelled through the air.

▼ Passing over a third – the ball must be caught or touched in the correct area. A free pass or throw-in is awarded at the point where the ball entered the incorrect area.

▶ This England player shows excellent passing technique.

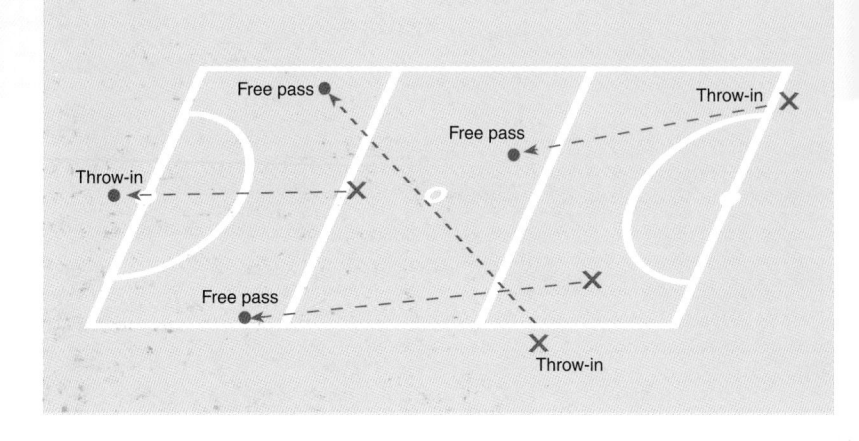

CONTROLLING SKILLS

Once competitive play starts, the skills of getting free and defending are required. As with the primary skills, these must combine good technique and the control required by the rules of netball, particularly those relating to obstruction and contact.

Defenders are in greater danger of obstruction because their aim is to 'stay close' to opponents while attackers attempt to 'get away'.

OBSTRUCTION

A player can cause obstruction if the arms are taken away from the body other than to provide natural balance.

Though obstruction is a fault, the rule identifies actions which are allowed as well as those which are not. Defending players may attempt to intercept or defend the ball, but must be standing a certain distance away from the player with the ball

before attempting to defend. This distance is measured on the ground and must be a minimum of 0.9m between one foot of the player with the ball and the nearer foot of the defending player.

The 'one foot' of the player with the ball is determined by that player's footwork when receiving the ball:

a. the landing, grounded or pivoting foot if it remains on the ground

Here the umpire signals for an obstruction.

b. the spot on the ground where the landing, grounded or pivoting foot was if it is subsequently lifted.

c. the nearer foot to the defending player if the ball handler lands on and remains grounded on two feet. If the player lands on two feet and lifts one, it is the foot still grounded that counts.

> **Umpires need to watch closely to check who is at fault when players are close, because attackers may be equally at fault in a contest for space or for the ball.**

DEFENSIVE OPTIONS

• From the correct distance, a defender may attempt to intercept or defend the ball by jumping towards the player with the ball. But the defending player commits obstruction if they land within 0.9m of the player still in possession of the ball.

• A player may defend an opponent who has chosen to go out of court. But the defending player cannot leave the court or their own playing area in order to defend.

• A defender can be within 0.9m of an opponent without the ball and may attempt to prevent that opponent from moving into space on court or moving to receive a pass. But all arm actions must be disciplined. The player will be penalised for obstruction if the arms are used as intentional barriers.

• A defender may be within 0.9m of an opponent in possession of the ball, provided that no effort is made to defend. The defender must control their movement and proximity because they cannot interfere with the opponent's throwing or shooting action.

ATTACKING OBSTRUCTION

Attacking players can be charged with intimidation, but can only commit obstruction when they are not in possession of the ball. They are bound by the same rules as close-marking defenders, so in close proximity their arm actions must be disciplined.

DEFENSIVE DEFAULTS

- Even at the correct distance from a player with the ball, a defender may not move forward to reduce the distance, including overbalancing (the defending player is not penalised if the player in possession of the ball lessens the distance).

- A defender cannot prevent a player who is legitimately out of court from re-entering.

- A player who is standing out of court cannot attempt to defend a player who is on the court.

- Any action that 'intimidates' an opponent is illegal. The umpire will intervene immediately when actions change from skilled effort to unpleasantness.

NOT OBSTRUCTION

No player is obstructing if the arms are outstretched to:

a. catch, deflect or intercept a pass or feint pass

b. obtain a rebound from an unsuccessful shot at goal

c. signal momentarily for a pass, or to indicate the intended direction of movement.

TRAINING TIP – KNOW THE OBSTRUCTION RULE

Players should know what the obstruction rule allows and limits. In a game, all players are attackers if their team is in possession of the ball and defenders if they are in opposition. Practise both attacking and defending actions with an awareness of the obstruction rule, even though you may play in a position that focuses on one or the other.

OBSTRUCTION AND CONTACT IN WHEELCHAIR NETBALL

Specific rules govern obstruction and contact situations for those playing wheelchair netball:

- No player should touch an opponent, an opponent's wheelchair or a ball held by an opponent so as to interfere with their play, either deliberately or accidentally.

- When the player is holding the ball, the distance on the ground between the nearest part of their wheelchair and the nearest part of an opponent's chair must be at least 1m.

- A player may position her- or himself closer than 1m to an opponent without the ball, but must not extend their arms except to intercept a pass.

A coach in a wheelchair advising players.

ATTACK AND DEFENCE

Attacking play is known as 'getting free' or 'dodging'. Defending play is referred to as 'marking'. This section contains plenty of tips to improve your attacking and defensive skills.

ON THE ATTACK

There are lots of different ways to play in an attacking manner.

- Get away from a close-marking opponent by using sudden dodging movements within a small space; running at full speed to outsprint an opponent; using body or step actions to change direction suddenly during a run, or to deceive an opponent before sprinting out.

- Use constant adjustment of position to 'hold space' in a chosen spot on court. Wait until team-mates are ready to respond to a signal indicating the direction of a forward run. Shooters use this skill often, though other players may use it for a free pass or a throw-in.

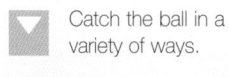
Catch the ball in a variety of ways.

- Watch team-mates to assess which are in a good position to receive the next pass, either because they are in clear space or will be seen easily by the receiver. Then move to receive the pass or to clear a position for a subsequent pass.

- Assess where to throw, choose the best throw and execute a successful pass.

IN DEFENCE

Defenders must at all times attempt to stop opponents receiving the ball in order to gain possession and start a counterattack. Defenders have two main aims:

- intercept the ball – catching or deflecting a pass intended for one of the attackers

- defend the ball – making throwing or shooting difficult for the attackers or causing a misdirected pass.

PENALTIES

This second aim leads to most obstruction faults by defending players. Umpires will be ready to penalise defenders who:

- are closer than the correct distance

- step forward in their attempt to take action

- jump forward and land near an attacking player who is still in possession of the ball

- intimidate the player rather than defend the ball.

BEST DEFENCE

To intercept a pass, stay very close to opponents; try to anticipate the timing of their dodges.

- Concentrate on reading where an opponent intends to move; use close marking and positioning to prevent an attacker's pathway into space, but be careful of obstruction.

- Be active in spaces slightly away from opponents to tempt a pass to what appears to be a 'free attacker', or to reduce options for attackers trying to move into space.

▲ This player makes good use of space to intercept.

KNOW THE LIMIT

Pushing, bumping, tripping, knocking, charging, holding or any other contact that impedes the play of an opponent are illegal.

AWARDING PENALTIES

Umpires will award a penalty if the player in an effort to attack or defend or to play the ball:

- moves into the path of an opponent who is committed to a particular landing space
- positions themselves so closely to an opponent that the player is unable to move without contacting
- places a hand or hands on a ball held by an opponent
- knocks or removes the ball from the possession of an opponent.

DISCIPLINE

Rule-governed behaviour and good spirit are expected from all players throughout the game, including during stoppages and dead ball situations. Umpires will apply the correct penalties for infringements but will also act against poor discipline. Rough or dangerous play is penalised as follows:

> Some contact is inevitable and is permitted if it does not interfere with the play of an opponent.

- the offending player is warned
- for further misconduct, the player may be sent off for a period decided by the umpire.

Sent-off players cannot be replaced, and can only return to the court once the suspension period has ended and following the scoring of a goal.

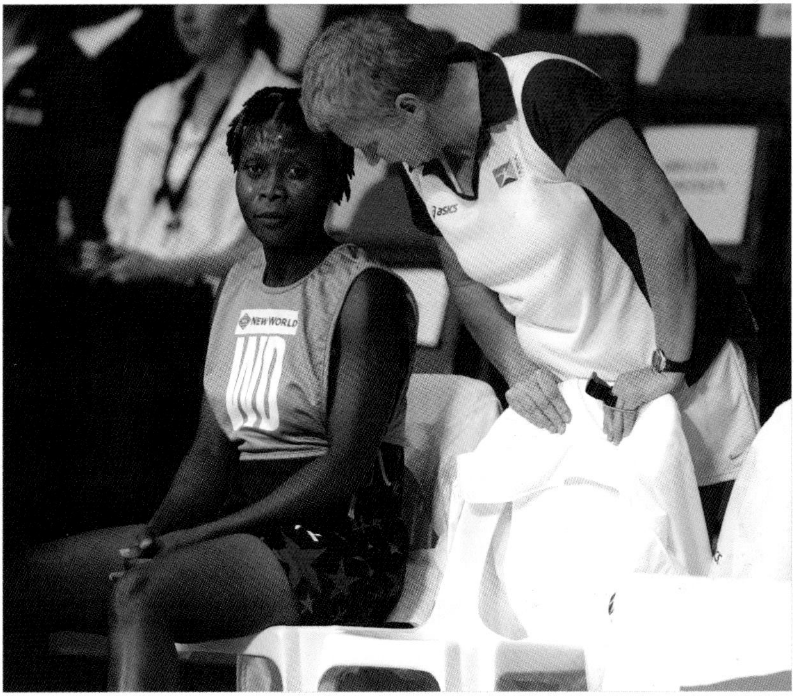

This player has been sent off during a World Championship match.

BASIC TRAINING

All attacking and defending skills should be practised with the aim of improving physical control. This will help players to do as follows:

- Play the game safely.
- Play the game within the rules, particularly those relating to footwork, obstruction and contact.

PLAY FAIR

Netball skills need to be precise, economical and disciplined and players must learn to execute these skills within the rules and in fairly restricted playing areas.

Learn the contact rule and practise to become stronger and faster, versatile and daring, without losing control, balance and precision.

CONTROLLING THE GAME

Umpires control the game with the assistance of other match officials. Playing faults are penalised in a number of different ways; this section focuses on free passes and penalty passes.

PENALTY PLAY

The penalties awarded for the breaking of rules are free pass; penalty pass or penalty pass/shot; throw-in; and toss-up. For quick reference:

- **A free pass** is awarded when another player is not involved (e.g. footwork penalties).

- **A penalty pass** (or shot) is awarded when another player from the opposition is involved (e.g. obstruction penalties).

- **A throw-in** is awarded when the player's foot is on the court before releasing the ball. Either another pass or penalty can be awarded depending on the circumstances (see page 50 for more detail).

- **A toss-up** is given when there is a simultaneous infringement (e.g. both players contacting to gain possession of the ball).

 This player is taking a penalty at the World Netball Championships.

During the 2007 World Championships, an English player attempts to win the ball from the Jamaican wing attack.

FREE PASS

A free pass is awarded for the following faults:

- when a single player is offside

- when a single player moves into the centre third before the umpire's whistle at the start of play

- for receiving a centre pass in the wrong area of the court

- when a shooter attempts a shot after being in contact with the ground outside the goal circle

- for all ball-handling faults

- for all footwork faults

- if a late arrival enters the game without following the proper procedures

- if an injured player returns to the vacant position in a game without following the proper procedures

- if a player ready for a toss-up moves before the umpire's whistle.

A toss-up is given.

The umpire determines where a fault occurred.

PENALTY PASS

A penalty pass is awarded for all actions that contravene the obstruction and contact rules.

- If given inside a goal circle, the shooters are offered a penalty pass or a pass/shot. The shooter may choose which to take and is not required to indicate their choice.

- A pass/shot is also awarded to the shooting team if a defender moves the goalpost in a way that interferes with a shot at goal.

Free passes are always taken close to where the offence occurred. For a penalty pass, an umpire may choose the spot where the non-offending player is standing if that player would be disadvantaged by taking the penalty where the offending player is standing.

FREE PASS VERSUS PENALTY PASS

- A free pass and a penalty pass are similar in that both involve a 'pass' taken by the non-offending team from the point where the offence occurred.

- In a penalty pass, the offending player has to stand beside and away from the thrower until the ball has left that player's hands.

- Other players are allowed to defend the pass, as with a free pass.

PENALTY PASS – EXAMPLE

A centre leans over the goal circle and makes contact with a shooter with the ball, which is a 'contact' fault. The offender is standing outside the circle, but the interference could have disturbed a shot at goal.

The umpire will award a penalty pass or penalty shot inside the goal circle rather than a penalty pass outside, evaluating the possible advantage or disadvantage to the non-offending team.

When a penalty shot is offered as an alternative, the same restriction is placed on the offender, i.e. stand beside and away from the shooter until the ball is released (note the centre must remain onside in this example).

When two offenders are involved in an incident, both must stand out until the ball is released. If defenders move too soon, the penalty is retaken.

A penalty pass being taken by the wing attack.

THROW-INS

A throw-in is awarded for all out-of-court infringements.

- For an infringement at a goal line, the throw-in is taken outside the court where the ball first crossed the line.
- At a sideline, a throw-in is taken where the ball first crossed the line.

THROW-IN INFRINGEMENTS

A throw-in is awarded for the following faults incurred by the team in possession while taking a throw-in:

- failure to ensure that all other players are on court before taking the throw-in
- failure to position correctly before taking the throw-in
- breaking the footwork or ball handling rules after taking up this position
- moving a foot onto the line or into court before releasing the ball
- stepping behind an offside area before releasing the ball.

Other faults that occur at a throw-in are as follows:

- the ball passes over a complete third of the court. The penalty is a free pass at the point where the ball entered the incorrect third

- obstruction or contact involving a defending player on court. Either player might be at fault. The penalty pass (or penalty pass/shot) is awarded to the non-offending team and is taken on court.

OVER OR OUT

- If the thrown ball fails to enter the court, a throw-in is taken by the opposition from the original spot.
- If the thrown ball travels across court and passes out, a throw-in is awarded to the opponents at the new spot.

TOSS-UP

A toss-up is awarded for all simultaneous offences by two opposing players:

- offside, with one or both having caught or made contact with the ball
- action causing the ball to travel out of the court
- contact that impedes play.

Whenever possible, it is required that the two players involved in the incident shall take part in the toss-up, either at the point where the incident occurred or as near as possible to that point on court and in an area common to both.

A toss-up is also taken to put the ball into play in the following situations:

- two opposing players gain possession of the ball at the same time, even if one of these players lands out of court

- after an accident if play stopped while the ball was on the ground or the umpire failed to note who was in possession of the ball at the moment play stopped

- the umpire cannot determine who last touched a ball that has gone out of court.

Exciting play during the International Netball Test Series.

TOSS-UP (Cont.)

The toss-up involves two opposing players.

- There must be a distance of 0.9m between the nearest foot of each player.

- Players may choose how to stand but must have their arms straight and hands at their sides.

- They must be facing their attacking goal end.

- They must remain still after the umpire has checked their positions until the whistle is blown, but can move their heads to watch the movement of the ball.

TOSS-UP – THE UMPIRE

The ball rests on the palm of the umpire's hand in the 'ready' position, just below the shoulder level of the shorter player's normal standing position.

Having checked the players' stance, the umpire moves forwards and, after a pause, blows the whistle and flicks the ball upwards. The umpire has to ensure that the ball is released mid-way between the two players, flicking it up not more than 60cm in the air when the whistle is blown.

THE UMPIRES

Two umpires are on court during a netball game, controlling the play and making decisions. In organised matches, they will be assisted by scorers and timekeepers.

Umpires as well as players are bound by the rules of netball, and must make decisions according to the rules of the game. Before a game begins, the umpires will make sure that playing conditions are correct, checking the equipment and players, particularly clothing.

The rules, and the umpires' responsibility in applying them during a game, are covered throughout this book. Umpires will start and stop a game, signal a successful goal and generally control the organisation of a game. When they spot a playing fault, they will blow a whistle and administer the correct penalty, so must have a thorough knowledge of all aspects of netball.

A free pass is awarded if a player moves in a toss-up. It may be taken by any onside member of the opposing team.

Here, the umpire is keeping a close eye on the game.

ADVANTAGE

Umpires can decide to allow the game to continue following a playing fault. This section explains when and why umpires will decide to 'play advantage'.

PLAY ON

Umpires are required to use their judgement before penalising playing faults. They should not blow their whistle in a situation where the non-offending team would be placed at a disadvantage, instead allowing the game to continue. Such decisions are not easy of course and the umpire must seek to strike a balance.

The most commonly applied advantage in the first stages of play relates to offside decisions, particularly where a single offside player does not have the ball. It may be that the non-offending team is already in possession and in a good position.

GETTING THE BALANCE RIGHT

When applied correctly, the rule on advantage gives umpires the power to ignore faults, letting a game flow without excessive interruption. Players and spectators prefer this. However, the umpire risks losing control of a game when too many faults pass unchecked or the players feel they can take advantage of an umpire's apparent non-involvement.

Future international players compete for the ball!

PLAY-ON EXAMPLES

Many obstruction incidents can be left unpenalised by umpires, although they will signal advantage. Here are two incidents:

1. the speed of an attacking player's landing and subsequent pass are in no way interrupted by a close-marking opponent who has no time to move away to the required 0.9m

2. a shot at goal is successful in spite of the defence stepping in towards the shooter.

In both cases, it is unnecessary to stop the game, and may positively disadvantage the attacking team to have a successful pass or shot ignored in order to take a penalty.

Only experienced umpires will play advantage in more debatable and subtle situations in addition to the obvious and uncontroversial ones described here.

FINAL WORDS

Use the information on rules and tips on technique to improve your netball skills. If you are unsure about any of the rules, you can check them at the addresses listed in the front of this book and on pages 56–57.

You may be sent off for rough and dangerous play, or misconduct, so play the game in a good spirit at all times. Respect your opponents, play safely, accept the umpire's decision and above all, enjoy the game.

Play netball in a good spirit.

CONTACTS

The England Netball Website

The All England Netball Association is the governing body of netball in England. If you would like any information regarding netball in England please visit the England Netball website:

www.englandnetball.co.uk.

England Netball's Regional Units

If you interested in playing netball and/or want to know what is happening in your area, please visit your region's website. Alternatively you can email or call the regional office.

North West: www.netballnorthwest.org.uk
Email: northwest@englandnetball.co.uk
Tel: 01925 534333

North East: www.northeastnetball.co.uk
Email: northeast@englandnetball.co.uk
Tel: 0191 3347223

Yorkshire: www.netballyorkshire.co.uk
Email: yorksandhumber@englandnetball.co.uk
Tel: 0114 223 5669

West Midlands:

www.westmidlandsnetball.moonfruit.com
Email: westmidlands@englandnetball.co.uk
Tel: 01902 518 752

East Midlands:

www.eastmidlandsnetball.co.uk
Email: eastmidlands@englandnetball.co.uk
Tel: 01509 226753

East: www.netballeast.org.uk
Email: east@englandnetball.co.uk
Tel: 01953 606 063

London and South East:

www.londonandsoutheastnetball.co.uk
Email: londonandsoutheast@englandnetball.co.uk
Tel: 01895 266 202

South: www.netballsouth.co.uk
Email: south@englandnetball.co.uk
Tel: 01628 477090

South West: www.netballsouthwest.co.uk
Email: southwest@englandnetball.co.uk
Tel: 01225 383774

The Co-operative Netball Superleague

Visit the Superleague franchises website to get an update of all the latest information on the teams. It's packed with information regarding the team players, where and when they are playing, latest scores and photos.

www.brunelhurricanes.co.uk – Brunel Hurricanes

www.welshnetball.co.uk – Celtic Dragons

www.leedsmet.ac.uk – Leeds Carnegie

www.loughboroughlightning.co.uk – Loughborough Lightning

www.mavericksnetball.co.uk – Mavericks

www.thundernetball.com – Northern Thunder

www.teambath.com – TeamBath

www.teamnorthumbria.com – Team Northumbria

www.glasgowwildcats.co.uk – Glasgow Wildcats

General Netball and Sport Websites
Visit these websites for general information on netball.

www.worldnetballchamps.com – IFNA Netball World Championships

www.netball.org – International Federation of Netball Associations (IFNA)

www.netballireland.com – Netball in the Irish Republic

www.netballscotland.com – Scottish Netball Association

www.welshnetball.co.uk – Welsh Netball Association

www.netballnz.co.nz – Netball New Zealand

www.netball.asn.au – Netball Australia

www.abc.net.au/netball – Netball Australia News

www.anz-championship.com – ANZ Championships

www.skysports.com/netball – Sky Sports Netball Pages

www.express.co.uk/netball – Daily Express Netball Pages

http://news.bbc.co.uk/sport – BBC Sport Netball Pages

www.womensportreport.com – Online magazine for all sportswomen

www.netballpost.com – Netball site for all levels

www.netballonline.com – The World Wide Netball Forum and Community

www.netballroadshow.co.uk – International Netball Roadshow

www.net-it.org – Junior Netball Coaching Camps by England & Superleague Players

www.sportrelief.com – Sport Relief

www.eis2win.co.uk/pages – English Institute of Sport

www.sportengland.org – Sport England

www.sportscotland.org.uk – Sport Scotland

www.uksport.gov.uk – UK Sport

www.sportscoachuk.org – Sports Coach UK

www.mencap.org.uk – Mencap Sport

www.bucs.org.uk – BUCS – British Universities & Colleges Sport (formerly BUSA)

www.britishcollegessport.org – BCS – British Colleges Sport

www.ucsport.net – British Universities & College Sport

www.ccpr.org.uk – Central Council for Physical Recreation (CCPR)

www.wsf.org.uk – Women's Sports Foundation UK

www.activeplaces.com – Active Places

GLOSSARY

Advantage When the umpire lets the game continue, following an infringement, if this benefits the non-offending team.

Attacking team The team in possession of the ball.

Bat To direct the ball with the hand towards a team-mate.

Centre circle The small circle in the centre of the court. This is where plays starts and restarts following a goal.

Centre pass The first pass taken to start or restart a game after a goal has been scored.

Contact Pushing, bumping, holding or any other physical action that interferes with an opposition player.

Court The area on which a netball game is played.

Dead ball When the game has been stopped by the umpire during regulation playing time.

Defending team The team that is not in possession of the ball.

Dodging Any means of getting away from an opponent.

Feint A pretend pass or move in one direction before moving in another.

Footwork rule The rule limiting the physical movement of a player in possession of the ball.

Free pass A pass given to the non-offending team for all infringements other than obstruction or contact.

Goal circle The semicircle marking the shooting area at each end of the court.

Goal line The boundary lines at either end of the court.

Intercept When a defender gains possession of a pass intended for an opponent.

Intimidate Behaving aggressively towards an opponent.

Marking Staying close to an opponent in order to prevent them from receiving a pass.

Obstruction When a defending player intentionally interferes with a pass or shoot.

Offside When a player ventures into an area of the court which is not within their playing area.

Onside When a player is within their playing area.

Out of court When a ball or player leaves the court.

Penalty pass A penalty given to the non-offending team for breaking the obstruction or contact rule.

Penalty shot As above; if the penalty occurs in the goal circle, a shooter may either pass or shoot.

Pivoting When a player keeps one foot firmly on the ground and swivels with the other foot.

Playing area The area of the court within which a player is allowed to move.

Rebound A jump to retrieve the ball after a missed shot.

Replay When a player attempts to catch, bat or bounce a ball after failing to complete a catch.

Sideline The lines running down each side of the court.

Throw-in Used to put the ball back into play when it has gone out of court.

Tip To direct the ball with the fingertips towards a team-mate.

Toss-up A penalty used to put the ball back into play when, for example, two opposing players have committed an offence.

Transverse lines The two lines across the court dividing it into thirds.

Umpires The two officials who are on court, making decisions and in control of the game.

NETBALL CHRONOLOGY

1891 Foundations are laid for women's basketball.

1895 First game of netball takes place at Madame Ostenburg's College, England following a visit by American Dr Toles.

1926 The All England Net Ball Association is established.

1935 Name changed to All England Women's Association for Net Ball and other Hand Ball games.

1944 Association now known as the All England Netball Association.

1949 England wins first international matches against Scotland and Wales.

1951 Silver Jubilee celebrated. Netball demonstrated at Festival of Britain Exhibition.

1956 First England team visits Rhodesia and South Africa.

1957 England beat The Rest at the Empire Pool, Wembley. First International Rules Conference held.

1959 South Africa tour England losing all three Test Matches.

1960 Inaugural meeting of International Federation of Women's Basketball and Netball Associations in Ceylon. The International code of rules is adopted.

1963 1st World Tournament, Eastbourne. England finish 3rd.

1967 2nd World Tournament, Australia. England finish 4th.

1970 Formation of English Schools Netball Association.

1971 3rd World Tournament, Jamaica. England finish 3rd.

1975 4th World Tournament, New Zealand. England finish 2nd.

1976 Celebrations held for the Association's Golden Jubilee.

1979 5th World Tournament, Trinidad. England finish 4th.

1983 6th World Tournament, Singapore. England finish 4th.

1985 World Games in London. New Zealand win, England finish 4th.

1987 7th World Tournament, Glasgow. England finish 4th.

1988 1st World Youth Cup, Australia. Australia win, England finish 2nd. A new English Counties league is launched.

1989 World Games in Karlsruhe. Australia win, England finish 3rd.

1991 8th World Championship, Australia. England finish 4th.

1992 2nd World Youth Cup, Fiji. New Zealand win, England finish 4th.

1994 English Schools Netball Association merges with the AENA after 25 years as a separate body. South Africa re-enters the international arena.

1995 9th World Championship hosted by England in its Centenary Year. Australia win, England finish 4th.

1996 3rd World Youth Championship, in Canada. Australia win, England finish 3rd.

1997 International Federation of Netball Associations Council Meeting in Barbados to consider rule changes.

1998 Netball is included in the Commonwealth Games for the first time in Kuala Lumpar. Australia win, England finish 3rd.

1999 10th World Championship, New Zealand. England finish 3rd.

2000 4th World Youth Championship, Cardiff. England finish 4th.

2001 AENA celebrates its 75th Anniversary. AENA Hall of Fame is also launched. The Racial Equality Charter for Sport is signed at the AENA Annual General Meeting.

2002 Commonwealth Games in Manchester. England finish 4th. AENA achieves preliminary award of the Racial Equality Standards for Sport.

2003 11th World Championship, Jamaica. England finish 4th.

2004 First Marion Smith Championships for Players with Learning Disabilities. TeamBath wins second Super Cup.

2005 5th World Youth Championship in Florida. New Zealand win, England finish 2nd. The Netball Superleague is launched.

2006 Commonwealth Games, Melbourne. England finish 4th. Refuge named as England's first official charity partner. Second season of Netball Superleague televised by Sky Sports.

2007 England defeat New Zealand for first time in 32 years, as part of a tri-series with New Zealand and Australia. 12th World Championships moved from Fiji to Auckland, New Zealand. Australia win, England finish 4th. TeamBath win the Netball Superleague.

2008 England beat Malawi in the home Co-operative International Netball Test Series. Mavericks win the Co-operative Netball Superleague.

2009 England beat Jamaica in the home Co-operative International Netball Test Series. 6th World Youth Championship in Cook Islands. TeamBath win the Co-operative Netball Superleague Grand Final.

INDEX